NAME: _____

GROW

COPYRIGHT © 2020 FRESHWATER PUBLICATIONS

All rights reserved. No part of this book shall be reproduced or transmitted in any form or by any means, electronic, mechanical, magnetic, photographic including photocopying, recording or by any information storage and retrieval system, without prior written permission of the publisher. No patent liability is assumed with respect to the use of the information contained herein. Although every precaution has been taken in the preparation of this book, the publisher and author assume no responsibility for errors or omissions. Neither is any liability assumed for damages resulting from the use of the information contained herein.

Tree image by Nikitina Olga/Shutterstock.com

ISBN 978-0-9993994-9-1

freshwater

Freshwater Publications
St. Bonifacius, Minnesota

1 3 5 7 9 10 8 6 4 2

Printed in the United States of America

TABLE OF CONTENTS

INTRODUCTION	3
HOW TO USE THIS DEVOTIONAL	4
1—FAITH STEPS	7
2—JESUS IS ALWAYS WITH YOU	11
3—P.A.P.E.R.	15
4—HOW DID I GET HERE?	19
5—THE GOOD SHEPHERD	23
6—HOPE	27
7—STRONG FAMILIES	31
8—THE 4 R'S TO FINDING JOY	35
9—ARE YOU CONTENT WITH YOU?	39
10—FILL YOUR TANK	43
11—STEP INTO THE WATER	47
12—FILLING IN THE GAPS	51
13—HOW WOULD YOU RESPOND?	55
14—MOUNTAIN-MOVING PRAYER	59
15—GLORY OF GOD	63
16—PRAYER OF JABEZ	67
17—BETTER TOGETHER	71
18—PAUSE	75
19—THE DOLDRUMS	79
20—A PICTURE OF HEAVEN	83
21—HELPING THOSE WHO HURT	87
22—FAITH, HOPE AND LOVE	91
23—CHASING A GOD-SIZE DREAM	95
24—LIVING WATER	99

25—THE TUMBLER 103
26—THE LIGHT OF THE WORLD 107
27—THE HOLY SPIRIT'S VOICE 111
28—CONNECTED TO THE VINE 115
29—SUFFERING 119
30—BELIEVE 123
31—THREE SPIRITUAL CATALYSTS 127

INTRO

> "You will make known to me the path of life; In Your presence is fullness of joy; In Your right hand there are pleasures forever."
>
> **PSALM 16:11**

INTRODUCTION
PASTOR JOHN BRALAND

James 4:8 says, *"Draw near to God and He will draw near to you."* We must have time with God and He asks us to make the first move by turning our hearts toward Him. As we turn our heart to Him, He reaches out to us like a loving parent with open arms and a warm smile.

The purpose of this devotional book is to help you draw closer to the heart of God by cultivating your relationship with Him. God wants your connection with Him at this heart level. It's accomplished by learning more about who God is, how He works, and how you can align your life to fulfill His purposes for you.

This devotional will point you to the scriptures and challenge you to apply them to your life. It's not a substitute for reading the Bible but a tool to help you go deeper by providing insights on key passages.

For the greatest benefit set aside 10-15 minutes every day to read through one of the devotions. Read it with the goal of getting to know God better. Before you start, pray that the Holy Spirit will help you to be teachable. Then read through the devotion and reflect by answering the questions that correspond with the theme of the day.

Each lesson is written to challenge you in a different way. When you are finished, spend a few more minutes in prayer and ask God to help you apply what you just learned to your life. Don't be surprised if God gives you the opportunity to apply what you just learned that same day.

The beauty of an intimate walk with God is that we can know His will (1 Corinthians 2:16), have our joy made full (John 15:11), and can expect our prayers to be heard and answered (John 15:7).

There is security, rest, and peace when we live a Christ-centered life. When we read God's Word, we see God's heart and how He wants our hearts (James 1:25), then devotions are meaningful and purposeful.

HOW TO USE THIS DEVOTIONAL
GUIDELINES FOR GROWTH

- Designate about 10-15 minutes of uninterrupted time each day.
- Read the daily devotional.
- Using the reflection questions, spend some time putting your thoughts on paper. Journaling is a spiritual discipline that can help you hear from God as you reflect on His power and presence in your life.
- Attend church. God delights in our gathering together to worship and grow through the teaching of His word. Come each Sunday to worship with us and deepen your understanding of scripture.

DAILY DEVOTIONALS

"Therefore, rid yourselves of all malice and all deceit, hypocrisy, envy, and slander of every kind. Like newborn babies, crave pure spiritual milk, so that by it you may grow up in your salvation, now that you have tasted that the Lord is good."

1 PETER 2:1-3

DEVOTIONAL 1
FAITH STEPS

When my son was very young, we gave him a trike. At first, he pedaled really slow and cautiously, but the more he rode it, the faster he wanted to go. Eventually he was so good at riding his trike that he wanted a two-wheeled bike with training wheels.

At his first time on the new bike my son was intimidated by it but determined to ride. I stood next to him and reassured him that he could do it. He sat on the seat and began to pedal. For a few weeks he rode around happy as could be. But then he wanted the training wheels off.

Again, his approach was timid because it was just him and two wheels. I couldn't ride it for him, I couldn't work the pedals—I could only give support and help him get his balance. This time there would be no crutch, no extra support, just a sweet hand-me-down blue Huffy. Ultimately my son had to decide whether to keep pedaling or hit the brakes.

With the training wheels off Josh swung his leg over the frame and put one foot on the pedal. I was behind him helping him balance, and my wife was 10 feet in front of him with open arms of reassurance that he could pedal to her. With a little push he pedaled, wobbling back and forth, eventually making it to his mother. We did this over and over, lengthening the gap between his mother and me until he could ride on his own. By the end of the day he was riding in circles all by himself and has never looked back.

The same is true in our spiritual life. We need to move from just knowing about Jesus to actually growing close to him. You are responsible to keep making progress in your faith. You determine if it grows or plateaus. God is always willing to help you, but it's up to you to let Him.

REFLECTION

- *Is there an area of spiritual growth toward which you can begin pedaling?*
- *Identify someone right now to whom you can reach out for support as you pedal.*

> "The thief comes only to steal and kill and destroy. I have come so that they may have life, and have it to the full."
>
> **JOHN 10:10**

DEVOTIONAL 2
JESUS IS ALWAYS WITH YOU

John 10:10 records Jesus saying, *"The thief comes only to steal and kill and destroy. I have come so that they may have life and have it to the full."* Take note, He doesn't say rich and problem free—He says full. There is a huge difference.

If Jesus came to bring people a full life, why do bad things happen to good people? This is a very real and perplexing question.

During a regular meeting with a men's group we talked about what Jesus said. The son of one friend on the team was stillborn on Mother's Day in 2015, one week before his due date.

Another friend's wife has serious chronic, painful health problems. A third friend lost the majority of his eyesight and deals with pain every single day. My other friend in the group has severe, painful, debilitating problems with his intestines. I have also battled critical stomach problems for years.

In our discussion about Jesus' promise of a full life we realized that despite our treacherous problems and pitfalls God has not abandoned us. Jesus said that in this world we will have trouble because this world is not our home. My friend, He is right.

The heavier the burdens you carry, the more critical it is for you to set your sight on Jesus and the promise of eternal life with Him. We will all face trials and troubles because we live in a sinful world that's full of good times and heartbreaking times.

Because we face these trials, an obstinate and reckless hope must be cultivated. The hope is that the Holy Spirit is here with us every day and that beyond death, we will be in the presence of Jesus every day into eternity.

"And we believers also groan, even though we have the Holy Spirit within us as a foretaste of future glory, for we long for our bodies to be released from sin and suffering. We, too, wait with eager hope for the

day when God will give us our full rights as his adopted children, including the new bodies he has promised us." Romans 8:23

If you think that living a full life means health and wealth, you will be sadly disappointed. God never promised this. He promises a full life, a life of purpose and significance in relationship with him.

God is with you in the most beautiful, bright moments life has to offer as well as in the disillusioning, painful and dark moments. He is celebrating when you are celebrating and weeping when you are weeping. God is with you. The key is that no matter how significant the trial, you are never alone.

Focus on Christ and trust Him to carry you through it, deliver you from it, or lead you around it. If you are a believer, the Holy Spirit resides within you and empowers you to stay strong.

Set your eyes on Jesus and live the full life that He offers. Trust Him whether you are in the pits or at the peak.

REFLECTION

- *Have you found it hard to fully trust that Jesus is with you, especially in the dark times?*
- *Is trusting Jesus just "mind over matter"?*
- *What are some steps you can take to cultivate or grow your trust in Him?*

"This, then, is how you should pray: 'Our Father in heaven, hallowed be your name, your kingdom come, your will be done, on earth as it is in heaven. Give us today our daily bread. And forgive us our debts, as we forgive our debtors. Lead us not into temptation but deliver us from evil.'"

MATTHEW 6:9-13

DEVOTIONAL 3
P.A.P.E.R.

My daughter Sara loves to make soup. Her first attempt didn't have any flavor because it consisted of boiled potatoes and carrots with no seasoning. Being the good father I am, I ate it. I tried to be encouraging, but we both knew it lacked something.

The second time Sara made soup, she added an entire cup of seasoning salt to her potatoes and carrots. She was getting closer, but this had way too much seasoning salt to even attempt consumption.

Sara kept at it and little by little she added the right ingredients in the right portions and cooked it for just the right amount of time—some potatoes, a few carrots, a fair amount of chicken, chicken bouillon, a touch of seasoned salt and...voila! The best soup in the world!

Our spiritual life is like a recipe. In order to grow in our faith, we must incorporate different ways to fellowship and worship in connecting with Christ—all in proper ratios.

The base of your spiritual walk might be attending church and reading devotional books, but without prayer, it isn't going to "taste" right.

I am convinced that through prayer God's power can change circumstances and relationships. God's power can help you face every problem, fight every battle, and finish strong. I believe that God can heal physical disease, emotional distress, remove marital obstructions, and meet financial needs.

Jesus' disciples intently watched Him pray and when He finished, they held their gaze at Him and said, "Lord, teach us to pray."

There was something so authentic, so transformative, so peaceful and powerful about Jesus' prayer life that even the people closest to Him asked for advice on how to pray. He gave it in Matthew 6:9-13.

To regain the power of prayer in your life, utilize the prayer pattern Jesus teaches in Matthew 6:9-13. Jesus didn't tell us to recite this prayer over and over. He says this is how you should pray, not what you should pray.

In His prayer Jesus reveals how to have a deeper connection with God in your prayer life. I created an acronym based on this prayer to energize my prayer life. The acronym is PAPER and it comes from this passage.

P—for Praise. *"Our Father in heaven, hallowed be your name."* When we praise God, we worship Him for who He is—for being awesome, powerful, righteous and just. We praise Him for His love, forgiveness, and grace.

A—for alignment. *"Your kingdom come, your will be done on earth as it is in heaven."* Prayer for alignment is asking the Holy Spirit to help us align our lives with God's precepts revealed in His Word, the Bible.

P—for provision. *"Give us today our daily bread."* Pray for your needs and wants. There is no request too big or too small for God. I open up my life and needs to God by sharing my aches, pains, and problems with Him.

I also share my hopes and dreams with Him because God knows me inside and out. God wants me to pray for my specific needs.

E—for exoneration. *"Forgive us our debts as we also have forgiven our debtors."* When we pray for exoneration, we are asking God to forgive us of our sins and help us to forgive others.

R—for rescue. *"And lead us not into temptation but deliver us from the evil one."* We need God to rescue us from the temptations we face. All of us face temptations and the Holy Spirit gives us the power to resist them.

Romans 8 talks about living by the power of the Spirit and how to tap into it to get through your challenges. Jesus wants us to come to Him as real and as transparent as we can be.

It is possible to integrate the practice of prayer into the rhythms of our lives.

It is possible to grow closer to Christ and deepen our love for Him and knowledge of Him.

It is possible to pray expectantly, trusting God to answer, even if His answer isn't what we expected. When you pray, think of the acronym PAPER to help you connect with God on a deeper level.

REFLECTION

- *20 seconds—can you memorize the acronym? Praise, Alignment, Provision, Exoneration, Rescue.*
- *Take a moment to construct a prayer today using PAPER and see how "Construction PAPER" strengthens your prayer life!*

> "God has delivered me from going down to the pit, and I shall live to enjoy the light of life."
>
> **JOB 33:28**

DEVOTIONAL 4
HOW DID I GET HERE?

Have you ever been in a bad relationship and asked yourself "How did I get here?" Have you ever found yourself ten years into a job that you hate asking, "How did I get here?" Have you ever felt like your relationship with God was non-existent and asked yourself, "How did I get here?"

The book of Judges describes the life and times of Israel and its spiritual leaders, called judges, after they moved into the Promised Land under Joshua's leadership.

Joshua was an excellent leader and the people who followed him were faithful to God. His armies were victorious because they put God first and did what God told them to do. Because they honored God, He was their guide and protector. Then Joshua died.

Almost immediately the people stopped worshipping God. From that point life went downhill. The Israelites lost every battle they fought. Their homes were plundered and many of them were sold as slaves.

It was a drastic turnaround from what they had known—their good life in the good land had gone bad very quickly. At some point they must have wondered, "How did we get here?"

Each time they realized how far they had drifted from God they would cry out to Him. The Lord would send another judge who would guide the people and provide leadership. God didn't give them a king because He wanted to be their king. God is the Lord of lords and King of kings.

This is why He appointed judges to lead the people instead of a king. But as soon as each judge died the people again strayed away from God.

It happened with Joshua, then with Othniel, and with Ehud. While they were alive and leading, the people thrived. As soon as they died, the people drifted. This pattern continued throughout the entire book.

It was a cycle of sin, bondage, repentance, and devotion, followed by sin and bondage again.

"Whenever the Lord raised up a judge for them, he was with the judge and saved them out of the hands of their enemies as long as the judge lived; for the Lord relented because of their groaning under those who oppressed and afflicted them. But when the judge died, the people returned to ways even more corrupt than those of their ancestors, following other gods and serving and worshiping them. They refused to give up their evil practices and stubborn ways." Judges 2:18-20

Even though God's people were living in God's Promised Land they were not living like spiritual people. They may have been physically where God wanted them to be, but their hearts were still in the wrong place. Even the greatest people can lose focus and wind up far from God. If it could happen to God's people who lived in the Promised Land, it can happen to God's people who fill the church.

The question is, how long will it take for you to cry out to God? Will it take a marriage crisis? A health crisis? A financial crisis? God does not create all the crises that we have but He can and will use them to help us develop greater dependency on Him.

Here is the key—if you find yourself in a place you should not be, don't keep going in that direction expecting things to change. Stop, and seek God. Ask Him for wisdom and guidance. Ask Him for strength. Don't wait twenty years like the Israelites. Don't get hung up on guilt, shame, and regrets, wondering how you got where you are. Just focus on going to where God wants you to be.

When God's people cry out, God becomes present. He shows up with peace, grace, love, and direction. Job endured some of the worst trials anyone could ever imagine and toward the end of his life he said *"God has delivered me from going down to the pit, and I shall live to enjoy the light of life."* Job 33:28

The Israelites were forced to ask, "How did I get here?" only after being forced into slavery and having their homes plundered. We need to be tenacious and intentional about growing closer to Christ every day so we will be less likely to gradually slip away from him. Take it one day and one decision at a time.

REFLECTION

- Is there an area of your everyday life (relationships, health, finances...) where you see a need to regain focus and draw nearer to Christ?
- Is there an obstacle that is hindering you from drawing nearer that you can boldly remove?

"I am the good shepherd; I know my own sheep, and they know me, just as my Father knows me and I know the Father. So I sacrifice my life for the sheep... They will listen to my voice, and there will be one flock with one shepherd."

JOHN 10:14-16

DEVOTIONAL 5
THE GOOD SHEPHERD

"And I will set over them one shepherd, my servant David. He will feed them and be a shepherd to them." Ezekiel 34:23.

In the Old Testament the Jews read this text with a prophetic understanding that God is the Good Shepherd who loves and cares for His people. Jesus also claimed to be the Good Shepherd knowing His sheep, declaring, *"I am the good shepherd; I know my own sheep, and they know me, just as my Father knows me and I know the Father. So I sacrifice my life for the sheep. I have other sheep, too, that are not in this sheepfold. I must bring them also. They will listen to my voice, and there will be one flock with one shepherd."* John 10:14-16.

Jesus, the Good Shepherd, knows His sheep and they know Him in the same way that his Father knows Him and He knows his Father. He sacrifices His life for the sheep.

The Good Shepherd proves his love for His sheep by laying His life down on the cross for them, and He calls them by name. The sheep are His believers. You are not here on this earth by some random chance; you have been placed here by God for a purpose and God knows your name. He knows your first name, middle name, and last name. He knows how to say it and spell it. God knows you better than you know yourself.

Jesus calls you by name for two reasons. First, He calls you by name because He loves you and wants to have a relationship with you. Having a relationship with God is just like having a healthy relationship with another human being. When you become close to another person you call them by their first name because it is personal.

This is the significance of Jesus calling us by name. We are not just another human on earth. God came in the flesh as Jesus Christ so we would understand this. It's hard to conceptualize a loving God if you think of God as some mystical force.

Jesus is God in the flesh, and because He is a person, we can easily visualize having a healthy relationship with Him.
Second, like a good shepherd Jesus calls you by name because He wants you to follow Him. This takes trust on your part. You can trust that God is leading you to the best place. If you don't trust God, you will struggle to follow Him because you will always think you have a better path to get where you want to go. Jesus always has the best plan, though.

In response to God knowing you and calling you, reflect on these questions: First, am I listening and am I willing to follow? During your times of prayer do you take time to meditate on His word and quiet your mind to hear His voice? I will tell you, if you expect to hear a booming, resounding voice you will be sorely disappointed after years of listening when you never hear it.

I have never heard God speak in an audible voice to me, but yet I have heard Him speak to me. God speaks to us through the power of the Holy Spirit to reveal Himself, His purposes, and His ways. He speaks through His written Word, the Bible, through prayer, circumstances, and other people.

The second question is: Am I willing to follow? Just because you know God is leading you or calling you to do something doesn't mean that you are always willing to follow. Jesus calls His followers and our response should be to follow Him. Why? Because he loves us and wants what's best for us.

In verse 27 Jesus states, *"My sheep listen to my voice; I know them, and they follow me."* This is a matter of trust. Do you trust God enough to follow Him? It's one thing to say you do, and another thing to actually do it.

The Good Shepherd loves you and wants to have a relationship with you. Listen for His voice today. Try to open your eyes, heart, and mind to be receptive to His voice. Remember that He speaks in many different forms and we need to be intentional about listening for Him. Then, trust Him to lead you because He is the Good Shepherd, and following Him will be the best thing you have ever done.

Reflection
Pray...

> *...that your eyes, heart, and mind will discern the Good Shepherd's voice through the power of the holy Spirit.*

> *...that you will be receptive and obedient, trusting him as the One who has a better plan for your life than you do!*

"Jesus told her, 'I am the resurrection and the life. Anyone who believes in me will live, even after dying. Everyone who lives in me and believes in me will never ever die. Do you believe this, Martha?'"

JOHN 11:25-26

DEVOTIONAL 6
HOPE

My son Josh went on a mission trip to Tanzania, Africa to visit churches and work with children. After that seven of them planned to climb Mount Kilimanjaro—which is 19,341 feet tall! This mountain is unique in that you don't need to scale any vertical rock walls. One side of the mountain has a long, gradual slope to the top.

Josh was told to buy the best shoes he could find because they would be a large factor in his climb. The roundtrip climb takes a total of 8 days.

After six grueling days of hiking, they reached the summit. It was an incredible moment for the team—full of high fives and smiles. The air is so thin at the summit that they could only stay at that elevation for 18 minutes before beginning their descent.

After a difficult six-day journey up and an 18-minute mountaintop experience, they spent two days hiking back down.

Upon returning to base camp, the team rested, then gathered for a celebratory dinner. At this dinner Josh met a very discouraged man who arrived at the base camp the day before. Tony had saved his money, trained to climb the mountain, and traveled from America, only to find that all of his gear had been stolen with no hope of replacing it.

Tony's friends managed to give him a little extra clothing and the Sherpas were willing to lend him walking poles and a backpack. But without hiking boots the rest of the gear meant nothing.

Since there was no possible way to get new hiking boots in time to begin their ascent Tony had lost all hope of fulfilling his dream of climbing Mt. Kilimanjaro. Twelve hours later his group would head up the mountain without him.

At dinner that evening Josh overheard Tony say that he wore a size

11 shoe. Without hesitation Josh took off his size 11 hiking boots and handed them to Tony. With tears filling his eyes Tony took Josh's Solomon hiking boots. They were the same type, brand, and size of hiking boots that had been stolen at the airport two days earlier. The only difference was that Josh's boots were in much better condition than Tony's had been.

Tony could hardly believe that a teenager he didn't even know was willing to give him the shoes off his feet so he could fulfill his dream. After celebrating, Josh went back to his room stocking-footed and Tony left with Josh's boots—hopeful, determined, and ready to prepare for his climb.

Two months after Josh returned home, he received his hiking boots by mail with a note that said, "Thank you, I made it to the top. Your friend, Tony." Josh brought hope to Tony with a pair of hiking boots.

Jesus brings hope in the form of an empty tomb and a resurrected Savior. *"Jesus told her, 'I am the resurrection and the life. Anyone who believes in me will live, even after dying. Everyone who lives in me and believes in me will never ever die. Do you believe this, Martha?'"* John 11:25-26

Jesus' words are as relevant for you and me today as they were when He spoke them to Martha. These words, this promise of salvation after our death on earth, brings hope. There is more to live for than just this day—there are infinite tomorrows!

Jesus says that anyone can have hope in salvation if they just believe in Him. Trust Him to be your Lord and Savior today and live with the deeply rooted hope that there is life beyond your days here on earth.

REFLECTION

How does the hope we have in Jesus compare to the hope that Josh gave Tony? Think of some descriptors:

- The hope Josh gave Tony was _____

_____

- The hope we have in Jesus is _____

"I have been reminded of your sincere faith, which first lived in your grandmother Lois and in your mother Eunice and, I am persuaded, now lives in you also."

2 TIMOTHY 1: 3-7

DEVOTIONAL 7
STRONG FAMILIES

In his second letter to his apprentice Timothy the Apostle Paul presented three great insights about cultivating a healthy spiritual environment at home. Paul wrote, *"I have been reminded of your sincere faith, which first lived in your grandmother Lois and in your mother Eunice and, I am persuaded, now lives in you also."* 2 Timothy 1:3-7 This one sentence gives us a perfect picture of three generations of Christians.

Timothy's grandmother Lois became a Christian and lived out so well that her daughter Eunice was influenced to become a believer. Then Eunice lived out her faith so that her son, Timothy also became a believer. Lois and Eunice had such an effect on Timothy that their lives were visible to Paul through Timothy. In other words, when Paul looked at Timothy, he saw Lois and Eunice's influence shining through.

Their example to Timothy begs a question of us. What kind of values and virtues are you cultivating in your kids? The first insight Paul provides is to be sincere. The Apostle Paul said both Eunice and Lois had "sincere faith." That means they acted out their belief system.

They believed in Jesus and believed what He said was true, so they did what He said to do. They forgave others, they shared of their material things, they helped strangers, and they chose to be servants.

Our children watch us and they act on what they see. When my kids were little, all three of them was simultaneously screaming before lunch one day. So rather jokingly I said, "Josh, shut your pie hole." Of course, he heard what I said, and like a parrot, issued the same command to his sister. She was now telling him to shut his pie hole and he was telling her to shut her pie hole; then Katie told both of them to shut their pie holes.

I instructed Josh not to say that phrase and he immediately told me to shut my pie hole. I had modeled something I didn't want mimicked.

Kids are like magnets—they will pick up anything you give them whether good or bad. I'm sure that Eunice and Lois were not perfect, but their faith was sincere and they modeled what they believed.

The second insight is to be consistent. Being consistent as a parent is tough. Any parent knows that being a good example isn't always easy. And any parent willing to teach their teenager proper boundaries with social media and good driving skills knows that it's hard to "walk the walk" consistently.

What we learn best as children are lessons transmitted through consistent actions and boundaries rather than by verbal instruction. What are you transmitting consistently to your kids or other impressionable kids or young adults?

The third insight Paul provides is to be a growing Christian. Paul mentions three generations here, and there's no indication whatsoever that any of them stopped growing. They kept growing and continued to produce spiritual fruit in their own lives, which then impacted and nourished others.

Jesus promises us we will grow if we stay connected to Him. *"I am the vine; you are the branches. If you remain in me and I in you, you will bear much fruit; apart from me you can do nothing." John* 15:5

Here are some practical ways you can cultivate a healthy spiritual environment in your home:
- Participate in a group with other growing Christians and model your devotion to Christ-like friendships.
- Share with them regularly your love for Jesus and how He is working in your life.
- Pray as a family and share the answers to those prayers with each other.
- Go to church and be enthusiastic about this time spent together.
- Serve others together.

REFLECTION

- What kind of role model are you to your children? If you don't have kids or your kids are grown, what kind of role model are you to others?
- Are you OK with the life you're living in front of your children, family, and friends?

"As the Father has loved me, so have I loved you. Now remain in my love. If you keep my commands, you will remain in my love, just as I have kept my Father's commands and remain in his love. I have told you this so that my joy may be in you and that your joy may be complete."

JOHN 15:9-11

DEVOTIONAL 8
THE 4 R'S TO FINDING JOY

Jesus says, *"As the Father has loved me, so have I loved you. Now remain in my love. If you keep my commands, you will remain in my love, just as I have kept my Father's commands and remain in his love. I have told you this so that my joy may be in you and that your joy may be complete."* John 15:9-11

There are four decisions you need to make in order to experience more joy in your life. First, *receive God's love unconditionally*. Jesus tells you that the Father loves Him and He loves you. Receive it unconditionally.

Don't tell yourself that God will love you more if you clean up your act. He already loves you and wants to help you grow closer to Him, you just need to trust Him.

Second, *repent often*. Repenting from sin is like taking out the trash. When you keep unconfessed sin in your heart it begins to stink up the rest of your life as well. When you take the trash out in your own life God fills you with joy.

Third, *regret less*. Joyful people don't dwell on missed opportunities; they look for new ones. Let the Holy Spirit lead you to opportunities to develop spiritually, fellowship with other Christians, and serve.

- Take the opportunity to attend that retreat or conference that has been on your heart, even though it might be hard to break away from your day-to-day life.
- Join that group that seems like it might be good for your spiritual health, even though you are a bit uneasy about opening up to strangers.
- Invite a friend who might need a listening ear to coffee with you, even if it means you need to find a babysitter.

These things honor God. When you go to bed at night you want to be able to fall asleep knowing that you made the most out of your day. There is joy in that.

Fourth, *release others*. In other words, forgive those who have hurt you. Forgiving others is not something you can do on your own. You may be able to successfully repress your anger, but you cannot grant forgiveness unless you know what it is like to be forgiven by Jesus yourself.

We don't forgive others to give them a free pass to get away with something, we forgive them to release ourselves from the pain they caused. There is joy in that.

- Joy comes from knowing that you matter to God.
- Joy comes from knowing God's got your back.
- Joy comes from knowing you are being held in the very hands of God.
- Joy comes from knowing that you are a friend of God. Joy is a supernatural gift that comes from being connected to Christ by the power of the Holy Spirit.

In the worst moments of your life God will show up. Receive God's love, repent, regret less, and release others through forgiveness. This is where you will find joy.

REFLECTION

- Who can you release through forgiveness, right now and for good?
- Pray now for the Holy Spirit to reveal hidden sin; sometimes they are cleverly camouflaged as good when they are actually separating us from God.
- Take a minute to formulate a counter-statement for yourself for when you begin to dwell on your favorite regret.

"You made all the delicate, inner parts of my body and knit me together in my mother's womb. Thank you for making me so wonderfully complex! Your workmanship is marvelous— how well I know it. You watched me as I was being formed in utter seclusion, as I was woven together in the dark of the womb."

PSALM 139:13-15

DEVOTIONAL 9
ARE YOU CONTENT WITH YOU?

Your self-perception has a profound impact on your physical, emotional, relational, and spiritual well-being. If your perception is that you need to be perfect it impacts everything. You will always struggle with discontentment. There are three truths that you need to know and understand.

First, you are God's creation. In the very first book of the Bible, when God was creating everything, we are told that God created humans. You didn't evolve from a plant or an ape. You were purposefully created by God.

"Then God said, 'Let us make human beings in our image, to be like us.' So God created human beings in his own image. In the image of God he created them; male and female he created them." Genesis 1:27

Mom and dad might not have planned you, but you are no accident. God knew you were coming, and when you were in the womb, He took joy in you.

"You made all the delicate, inner parts of my body and knit me together in my mother's womb. Thank you for making me so wonderfully complex! Your workmanship is marvelous—how well I know it. You watched me as I was being formed in utter seclusion, as I was woven together in the dark of the womb." Psalm 139:13-15

When I first found out I was adopted, I thought I was a mistake. My adoptive parents were so good in telling me the truth and letting me ask questions about my biological parents. They told me over and over that I was not a mistake. I am able to believe them because I know it's true. God says so.

To this day, I have no idea who my biological parents are and probably never will. Regardless, I know I am not an accident, and neither are you.

Second, God created you for a purpose. He knew you were coming, and even before you were born, He recorded every moment of your life in His book. *"You saw me before I was born. Every day of my life was recorded in your book. Every moment was laid out before a single day had passed."* Psalm 139:16

Jeremiah was a prophet of God who was called to tell people to repent from their sins. For the most part his message fell on deaf ears. He was ridiculed, teased, thrown into a muddy cistern, anticipating he would be there until he starved to death. He battled depression on a personal level and often questioned if God knew what He was doing.

When Jeremiah was about 12 years old, God told him that he created him: *"I knew you before I formed you in your mother's womb. Before you were born I set you apart and appointed you as my prophet to the nations."* Jeremiah 1:5

Jeremiah clung to these promises when he felt discouraged and tempted to believe the lies others were saying about him. It must have been very hard to reject their words. But he clung God's truth that his life mattered and he had a purpose.

God used Jeremiah in a profound way to share His love with non-believers. *"For we are God's masterpiece. He has created us anew in Christ Jesus, so we can do the good things he planned for us long ago."* Ephesians 2:10

The third truth is that God is proud of what He made. *"How precious are your thoughts about me, O God. They cannot be numbered! I can't even count them; they outnumber the grains of sand! And when I wake up, you are still with me!"* Psalm 139:17-18.

Contentment comes when you understand that you were created by God, for a purpose, and that He is proud of what He made. You are no accident.

REFLECTION

- Do you believe there is a reason and a purpose for your existence?
- Is your answer based on the value put on you by others or is it based on the fact that you are already invaluable to the one and only Creator?

"There is a time for everything, and a season for every activity under the heavens:

a time to be born and a time to die,
a time to plant and a time to uproot,
a time to kill and a time to heal,
a time to tear down and a time to build,
a time to weep and a time to laugh,
a time to mourn and a time to dance,
a time to scatter and a time to gather,
a time to embrace and a time to refrain,
a time to search and a time to give up,
a time to keep and a time to throw away,
a time to tear and a time to mend,
a time to be silent and a time to speak,
a time to love and a time to hate,
a time for war and a time for peace."

ECCLESIASTES 3:1-8

DEVOTIONAL 10
FILL YOUR TANK

Many of us with full schedules somehow still live empty lives. The commitments we feel obligated to keep consume our calendar, and we try to squeeze every minute out of every day. Unfortunately, nobody can sustain this pace indefinitely. You will burn out from emotional and physical exhaustion, blow up in anger and frustration, or self-destruct from poor decisions.

We are the weakest and most vulnerable when we are most empty. In busy times like these you realize you cannot fill others when you are running on empty yourself. Here are six suggestions to fill your tank:

1. Keep a Sabbath day

It really doesn't matter what day you choose to rest, just pick one to retreat from the crazy and recharge your batteries. This isn't pop psychology; it's a biblical principle given to us by God.

2. Keep a realistic schedule

When you schedule your week, consider drive times and add some margin in between meetings, activities, and appointments. Plan times to do nothing at least once or twice a day just to give yourself some margin.

3. Know your limits.

Most people can handle only one emotional event a day. If you have emotionally taxing events multiple times every day you need to figure out how to relieve the pressure in a healthy way. You may need to exercise more, find even 30 minutes of alone time, or hand some stress off to someone else. Once you know your limits, don't overstep them.

4. Know your spouse's limits

My wife and I run at different paces. For a long time, I tried to nag her to go faster and she nagged me to slow down. I would want to invite people over but she would want to go out with friends. It seemed we couldn't get in sync on this, which meant neither of us were happy about it. Our solution was to communicate more and respect each other's limits. My wife now respects my pace and I respect hers. Once we accepted the reality that we run at different speeds we were able to pick the correct lane on the track and still finish together.

5. Schedule fun

We all need fun in our lives, but when we get busy fun is the first thing to go. Plan fun things to do as a couple, a family, or with a friend. Give yourself permission to have a good time and enjoy every second of it.

6. Invest in life-giving relationships

Chances are good that some people in your orbit suck the life out of you. It may even be your kids! All of us have people who deplete us. But for our own health we need to prioritize and invest an equal amount of our time in someone who completes us.

I have lunch once a week with a good friend just because he fills my tank. No matter how busy I am or how busy he is, we prioritize our time together. I always feel better after we meet, even if we don't talk about anything important.

If you want to live a full life, you need to have a full tank. And the only way to have a full tank is to fill it often.

REFLECTION

- *Write down this list and put it somewhere you can see it.*
- *If there are tank-fillers on the list that you could be more intentional about doing, plan them into the week ahead. Share your plan with someone who will help you remember to stick to it!*

> "Consecrate yourselves, for tomorrow the Lord will do amazing things among you."
>
> **JOSHUA 3:5**

DEVOTIONAL 11
STEP INTO THE WATER

Moses' successor, Joshua had seen God deliver the Israelites, providing them with food, protection, and direction again and again. After Moses died, one of the first things Joshua had to do was lead the people into the Promised Land. The problem was that the Jordan River was between them and their destination. They had no boats, the water was too deep to wade across, and too far to swim, especially since it was flooded at that time of year.

God could have easily stopped the water like He did for Moses. He could have provided a thousand boats or even erected a bridge for the people to cross, but He didn't. Instead, He let the river flow and gave Joshua some instructions to follow. The story is recorded in Joshua chapter 3 and points out three acts of faith.

First, keep their eyes on God.

"After three days the officers went throughout the camp, giving orders to the people: "When you see the ark of the covenant of the Lord your God, and the Levitical priests carrying it, you are to move out from your positions and follow it. Then you will know which way to go, since you have never been this way before." Joshua 3:2-4

The Ark of the Covenant was a chest made of acacia wood, overlaid with pure gold inside and out. It was 3'9" long and 2'3" wide and high. It contained the stone tablets with the Ten Commandments written on them, and some manna. This was the place where the Presence of God dwelled. It was the Israelites' most holy object and represented the living God.

Joshua told the people that when they saw the Ark pass in front of them, carried by the Levitical priests, they needed to follow it. Their first act of faith was to keep their eyes on God (the Ark) and move when He moved.

Second, expect something amazing to happen.

"Joshua told the people, 'Consecrate yourselves, for tomorrow the Lord will do amazing things among you'." Joshua 3:5

The people needed to have faith that God would answer their prayers. The Ark passed by and the people followed. When the priests came to the river, it was still flowing. All the people were looking ahead at an impossible situation while Joshua was trying to earn credibility. Now it was up to God.

Third, stand in the water without any promise that it will stop flowing. *"And as soon as the priests who carry the Ark of the Lord—the Lord of all the earth—set foot in the Jordan, its waters flowing downstream will be cut off and stand up in a heap."* Joshua 3:13

Only after they stepped in the water did it stop flowing. God could have stopped it prior to their arrival. He could have parted it like He did for Moses. But He didn't. He told the priests to step in without any reassurance other than His promise. Only after they got wet did the water stop. Then the people were finally able to cross over on dry ground.

The path of life ahead of you may at times look impossible to cross. Too many trials, too many obstacles, too big of a task, too many naysayers, lack of confidence...the list goes on. Most of us want the water to stop flowing before we step in. We want to have proof before we take the plunge.

A follower of Christ must trust that God can and will move the mountains in their life. They trust that, if they step out in faith, He will make a way for them. Sometimes we need to get our feet wet before God parts the water. Don't be afraid to step in the water, God will show up.

REFLECTION

- In your desire to see God move a mountain in your life, have you stalled out on one of the first two steps mentioned above?
- Is there a step of faith that you can take to "get your feet wet" and demonstrate your reliance on God to show up?

"And the King will say, 'I tell you the truth, when you did it to one of the least of these my brothers and sisters, you were doing it to me!'"

MATTHEW 25:40

DEVOTIONAL 12
FILLING IN THE GAPS

Years ago, Kathi and I moved a house and rebuilt it on a beautiful new location. After finishing the construction of the house, we put our focus on the landscaping. The first thing I did was build a rock retaining wall to stop mud flowing into our driveway every time it rained. Since I am too cheap to buy sod, I bought a bag of seed to spread around on the dirt, hoping to reap a lush green lawn. A month and a half later the lawn looked promising.

One day when the kids had their friends over, they decided to ride the four-wheeler, go cart, and golf cart around and around my yard. When they were done riding my newly sprouted lawn was gone.

Later that night while the kids were inside watching TV I was outside standing on black dirt, mourning. The grass was worn down to the dirt and the beautiful lawn that I had cultivated looked sorry and dry. The dirt was lifeless. It was beaten down and exhausted.

That reminds me of how many of us might be at the end of our work week. When we start the week, we may feel healthy and full of life. But after five days of problem solving, deadlines, family issues and relentless pressure, it may seem like we've been run over again and again and again. And by Friday we are as shredded as my lawn.

The question is, how do you fill in the gap between Monday and Sunday? Do you keep spiritually charged throughout the week so that you don't feel so run down and beat up by the end of it? How do you not only survive the week, but thrive?

Filling the gap between Monday and Sunday can begin when we commit to these five basic spiritual practices:

1. **Read the Bible often.** The Bible is God's written Word. 2 Timothy 3:16 declares, "*All Scripture is inspired by God and is useful to teach us what is true and to make us realize what is wrong in our*

lives. *It corrects us when we are wrong and teaches us to do what is right."* If you are new to reading the Bible, I suggest you start in the Gospel of John. Then read the book of Acts to give you a picture of how the early church grew. If you are struggling, read Philippians. Find a book in the New Testament (besides Revelation) and read one or two chapters a day.

2. **Pray daily.** Jesus' disciples asked Him to teach them how to pray. His instructions are given in the book of Matthew. Go ahead and turn to chapter 6 and read verses 7-13. Pray in the morning, throughout the day, and before you go to bed. The purpose of prayer is to connect your heart to God's heart, not to recite words. Talk to Him like a friend.

3. **Connect with other believers.** I am in a small group and love it. We meet every week to learn together, pray for each other, and enjoy one another's company. When we connect with other believers we are strengthened. Find a group of other Christians to connect with, or at least one or two friends who will pray for you and support you as you do the same for them.

4. **Serve like Jesus.** Serving others connects our hands and feet to the cause of Christ. Jesus said, *"And the King will say, 'I tell you the truth, when you did it to one of the least of these my brothers and sisters, you were doing it to me!'"* Matthew 25:40. Serving is important to Jesus because it helps others know that Jesus loves them and that those who believe in Christ care for and desire to serve others.

5. **Live generously.** The Apostle Paul wrote, *"Remember this: Whoever sows sparingly will also reap sparingly, and whoever sows generously will also reap generously."* 2 Corinthians 9:6. Everything in this world is destined for the dump, so don't get consumed with consuming. Learn to live within your means and live generously.

Don't read these five spiritual practices as a to-do list—read them as guidelines. They will help you to stay connected to Christ and growing as a believer. If you focus on these five practices and try to improve in them little by little, you will begin to fill in the gap between Monday and Sunday. You will not only survive each week but thrive. As for my lawn, I replanted and it regrew. After all, I'm raising kids, not grass.

REFLECTION

- Are you in the midst of a gap, feeling spiritually a little parched? Choose one of the suggestions outlined above to fill this gap at this time.
- Is there another gap-filler that you could employ more regularly? What would it take to do so?

> "I am the light of the world. Whoever follows me will never walk in darkness but will have the light of life."
>
> **JOHN 8:12**

DEVOTIONAL 13
HOW WOULD YOU RESPOND?

It was the last day of the Feast of Tabernacles. Jesus stood in the middle of a crowd at the temple in Jerusalem in front of the giant torches that were used to light the entire city. He declared, *"I am the light of the world. Whoever follows me will never walk in darkness but will have the light of life."* John 8:12

His bold claim provoked three responses from the people who heard Him. The first response was to challenge Jesus. The Pharisees said, *"Here you are, appearing as your own witness; your testimony is not valid."* John 8:13. According to the Law of Moses there must be two witnesses to make a legal claim, so the Jews tried to trap Jesus with a technical foul.

The Pharisees wanted to point Jesus to the law, but He said that His heavenly Father testifies on His behalf. He was sent to fulfill the prophecies because He is the Messiah. It is wildly popular to question Jesus' claim to deity. Books have been written to dispute His existence, His authority, His miracles, and His perfect life. In spite of all the attacks and all the interrogations and investigations, God's Word stands true.

The second response was to argue against Jesus' claim. Jesus claimed that God is His father. The Jews claimed Moses as their father. They were looking at their physical blood line and Jesus was talking on a spiritual level. So, they accused Jesus of being demon possessed. *"At this they exclaimed, 'Now we know that you are demon-possessed! Abraham died and so did the prophets, yet you say that whoever obeys your word will never taste death. Are you greater than our father Abraham? He died, and so did the prophets. Who do you think you are?'"* John 8:52

People still want to argue against Jesus today. Many want Jesus out of public schools and off public property. They want him out of courthouses even though our entire legal system is based on Judeo-Christian ethics. People are still trying to kill Jesus and twist every truth He taught. I have never met a happy atheist. There may be some out there, but every atheist I have ever met is angry at a god they don't even believe in.

The third response was to draw closer to Him because of His claim. *"Even as he spoke, many believed in him."* John 8:30. Today people still respond by challenging Jesus, arguing with Him or drawing closer to Him. From experience, I can tell you that drawing closer to Christ is far more pleasurable than fighting against Him or challenging Him. Nobody has ever fought God and won. This isn't bad because God knows what's best for us and He wants us to prosper in the biblical sense.

"To the Jews who had believed him, Jesus said, 'If you hold to my teaching, you are really my disciples. Then you will know the truth, and the truth will set you free.'" John 8:31-32

If you want to experience true freedom, come to Christ. He is the light of the world providing freedom from legalism, shame, and guilt. He offers hope and healing from darkness and despair.

REFLECTION

- *Who are the nay-sayers you know personally that need to hear about this freedom?*
- *Are you struggling with the third response mentioned above? What attitudes might be getting in the way? (Shame... fear of how it might change you... not knowing enough about Jesus to be certain of His claims...)*

"The King will reply, 'Truly I tell you, whatever you did for one of the least of these brothers and sisters of mine, you did for me.'"

MATTHEW 25:40

DEVOTIONAL 14
MOUNTAIN-MOVING PRAYERS

People who don't pray or refuse to pray, miss out on the power, peace, and presence of God. God most definitely listens to prayers, answers prayers, and moves in response to prayers because prayer moves the heart of God. Jesus said, *"Truly I tell you, if you have faith and do not doubt, not only can you do what was done to the fig tree, but also you can say to this mountain, 'Go, throw yourself into the sea,' and it will be done. If you believe, you will receive whatever you ask for in prayer."* Matthew 21:21-22

Jesus used the term "mountain" figuratively. He wanted to convey that believers can be confident that our prayers carry great power. Our prayers are more than empty wishes or good thoughts. But in order for our prayers to have power, they need to be fueled by faith.

There are two principles that will help you to pray mountain-moving prayers. The first is to be connected to Christ at all times. If you are living far from God it's very hard to sense His presence or hear His voice. When we are connected to Christ, we have spiritual power. We receive the power to endure, change direction, press on, or respond in a million other ways.

My friend Van Johnson, my son Josh, and I went to visit our missionary friends in Papua, New Guinea. On the way back we stopped in Japan for a couple of days. During our stay there we rode the trains to get around. Every time I got on a train, I couldn't help but look up because suspended above me was a web of wires that resembled a spider's nest. They were low-hanging, open power lines.

The trains have mechanisms that reach up and touch the wires which provides power to the giant electric motors that power the train. I am no electrician, nor am I an engineer, but I do know that all the power for the train comes from the wires and the train needs to be in constant contact with the wires or they won't move an inch. John 15:5 says, *"I am the vine; you are the branches. If you remain in me and I*

in you, you will bear much fruit; apart from me you can do nothing."
John 15:5

All of our power comes from Jesus. He sustains us, strengthens us, gives us wisdom, and enables us to do and see things that we never thought possible. Through our connection to Christ we receive healing and direction.

The second principle to pray mountain-moving prayers is to keep your sight on Jesus, not the mountain. Your mountain might be cancer, it might be a wayward child, your marriage, finances, or any other seemingly unmovable object.

Everyone has mountains to climb in their lives and we can't escape that they are there. When we turn our gaze away from Jesus and onto the mountain, we lose sight of the Mountain Mover.

Florence Chadwick was a well-known endurance swimmer—the first woman to swim the English Channel in both directions. When Florence jumped into the water to swim twenty-one miles from Catalina Island to the coast of California a dense fog was settling in. She could hardly see the boats in her own party and several times sharks got close to her and had to be driven off with shotguns.

More than 15 hours later, numbed with the cold Florence asked to be taken out. Her mother and trainer, alongside her in a boat, said they were near land she could surely make it. In her exhaustion Florence could only see dense fog when she looked toward her goal. She was pulled from the water only a half mile from the California coast.

Two months later Florence tried the swim again. This time the water was just as cold and the fog had rolled in again. The difference then was her belief she could make it.

She chose to continue believing the shore was just ahead though she couldn't see it until her feet touched the sea floor of the water's edge. Florence beat the previous record by two hours.

God does hear you and will provide for you, often in ways you would never expect. My friends, trust God even if you can't see the shore, and pray mountain-moving prayers, believing with all of your heart that He is listening. Believe that God will provide for you each step of the way and He will.

REFLECTION

- Take a moment to thank God for being worthy of your trust as He works in ways you cannot yet see.
- What "mountain-moving" prayer can you offer up to God right now for your own or someone else's behalf?

"The heavens declare the Glory of God; the skies proclaim the work of his hands."

PSALM 19:1

DEVOTIONAL 15
GLORY OF GOD

I tend to be very practical in my faith. I love how-to lists, top-ten lists, and setting personal spiritual goals. I like to know what I need to get done so that I can after it. But every once in a while, I am reminded of the awesomeness of God, and that He is beyond the scope of any top-ten list.

In 1977 Congress approved funding for the Hubble telescope. After years of hard work scientists finally launched it into space in 1990. Unfortunately, the first images they saw were blurry.

After months of trouble shooting engineers discovered that one of the reflective lenses was off by a fraction of a millimeter which caused blurring of the images. Three years later, in 1993, NASA sent a crew up to fix the lens. When the first pictures came back, they were even more astounding than scientists had imagined!

Because of the telescope scientists are able to see millions and millions of stars and other galaxies filled with planets. And as far as scientists can tell none of them are just like earth, able to sustain life. We are unique in every respect to the characteristics where life can exist.

David writes, *"The heavens declare the glory of God; the skies proclaim the work of his hands."* Psalm 19:1

What blows me away is the fact that God created all of this, yet He still knows my name! He knows yours too. The God who created the heavens and all of the earth wants to bless your life with His presence and purpose.

As stated by Joe Crews in his book *Amazing Wonders of Creation,*

"What would this planet be like without its restful carpet of living green grass and foliage? God did not have to clothe the ugly, bare soil with such a covering. Functionally, there needed to be no bright colors. Human beings could have survived on a bleak planet of gray ground and colorless plants. But they could not have survived as happily.

The Creator Himself was not only a lover of beauty; He loved His creatures so much that He wanted them to be happy, too. That's why He draped the earth with a half-million varieties of contrasting blossoms and leaves. And hidden inside each tiny bud, God placed secrets that would challenge the genius of earth's greatest scientists."

*Crews, Joe, *Amazing Facts, Inc.,* 2007, Amazing Facts. Web. 02 Sep 2016.
www.amazingfacts.org/media-library/book/e/1/t/amazing-wonders-of-creation

REFLECTION

- *What else in God's creation blows your mind and swells your heart with reverence and awe?*
- *Look for the next opportunity to speak of this amazing example of God's glory!*

"Jabez was more honorable than his brothers. His mother had named him Jabez saying, 'I gave birth to him in pain.' Jabez cried out to the God of Israel, 'Oh, that you would bless me and enlarge my territory! Let your hand be with me and keep me from harm so that I will be free from pain.' And God granted his request."

1 CHRONICLES 4:9-10

DEVOTIONAL 16
PRAYER OF JABEZ

In the book of First Chronicles, in the middle of chapter four, tightly nestled between verses 7 and 11, you will find a prayer that has the potential to change your life. One must wonder why this short prayer is even in this book. It seems like an afterthought, inserted in lists of genealogies.

This prayer is significant for us. Although we may not use the exact same words or be so bold, when push comes to shove Jabez was praying for the very same things that you and I desire.

"Jabez was more honorable than his brothers. His mother had named him Jabez, saying 'I gave birth to him in pain.' Jabez cried out to the God of Israel, 'Oh, that you would bless me and enlarge my territory! Let your hand be with me, and keep me from harm so that I will be free from pain.' And God granted his request." 1 Chronicles 4:9-10

We don't really know much about Jabez—he was a descendant of David, the literal Hebrew translation of "Jabez" means "pain," and he was honorable. As you see, 1 Chronicles 4:9 reads, *"Jabez was more honorable than his brothers; and his mother called his name Jabez, saying, 'Because I bore him in pain.'"*

Jabez asks God, "Keep me from harm so that it might not bring me pain!" This is an irony worth noting. Jabez knew his name meant "pain" but he wanted nothing to do with it. He asks faithfully and expectantly that God deliver him from pain.

In Jabez's prayer his first request was for God to bless him. Jabez didn't ask for a six-figure income or 1,000 sheep or 500 acres of land. Jabez left the blessing details entirely up to God. He gave his life to God and said, "I don't care how you bless me, I just want to be blessed by you." He knew the blessings God would create would be greater than he could ever imagine.

Second, Jabez asked God to enlarge his territory. He was not asking

God for more real estate. Jabez wanted more influence, more responsibility, and more opportunities to make a difference. He wanted to make an impact. He wanted God to use him to serve and touch the hearts of others.

Third, Jabez asked God to put His hand upon him. Jabez was faithful and showed humility in the presence of God. He had determination to fulfill God's will for his life. All that he needed was God's wisdom to know how to do that. That is where Jabez needed God's hand upon him—showing him the way by guiding him with His righteous right hand.

Fourth, Jabez asked God to keep him from harm. In the Lord's Prayer in the New Testament Jesus tells us to ask God to deliver us from evil. This is the same request. "Lord I pray that you will keep me from harm." Jabez knew that when God blessed him, expanded his territory, and put His hand on him, Satan and all his temptations would be very close behind.

Fifth, Jabez asked God to free him from pain. He was not praying that God would keep him from illness or emotional pain. He desired deliverance from the pain caused by sin. What am I talking about? The pain of having a guilty conscience. The shame and heaviness of the burden you carry around from the aftermath of sin.

Jabez was in the Old Testament before Christ, so his sins were not forgiven as they have been for you and me today. He had to endure the pain of his sin in a way we don't experience because of Jesus' sacrifice on the cross. Jabez prayed to be free from that immense pain.

At the end of the prayer the scriptures say God granted Jabez's requests. God blessed him, expanded his territory, put His hand upon him, kept him from harm and free from pain.

God wants to bless your life in ways unimaginable. He wants to use you in new ways. He wants to strengthen you to overcome challenges you could not without Him. He will give you crystal direction like never before. He wants you to experience His grace and mercy all over again.

REFLECTION

- *Highlight or underline the 5 statements above that describe Jabez's specific requests of God.*
- *How would those statements read if you expanded them into prayers on your own behalf, believing that God wants to bless you just as richly?*

"Since we are all one body in Christ, we belong to each other and each of us needs all the others."

ROMANS 12:5

DEVOTIONAL 17
BETTER TOGETHER

Do you remember the buddy system from school days? We used it when we went on field trips. Every student was assigned a buddy to make sure we didn't get lost or left behind. The Boy Scouts still teach the buddy system, as do many parents with their kids in crowded public places or vulnerable situations, like swimming.

The buddy system is referenced in the military by various names in each branch. The Air Force has "Wingmen," the Army has "Battle Buddies," and the Navy has "Shipmates." This system provides an effective measure of safety and accountability to leave no one behind.

The buddy system isn't just for school kids, Boy Scouts, and the military though; it's for us too. This becomes abundantly clear when we need help moving a couch or transporting our kids to an event. On a deeper level you may need a buddy to help you keep fighting a disease attacking your body, support you through heavy marital problems, or with the disappointment of a smashed dream.

The early church understood this need before it was called the buddy system. Writing to the Romans, the Apostle Paul said, *"Since we are all one body in Christ, we belong to each other and each of us needs all the others."* Romans 12:5. Let's face it—we need each other and are better together.

As Christians, our primary buddy system exists within the context of small groups. This is where deep friendships are formed, encouragement is given, and prayers are shared. Some powerful wisdom came from King Solomon, written in Ecclesiastes, chapter four, *"Also, if two lie down together, they will keep warm. But how can one keep warm alone? Though one may be overpowered, two can defend themselves. A cord of three strands is not quickly broken."* Ecclesiastes 4:11-12.

Who's watching your back right now, spiritually? Is there anyone in your life who is so close that they can help make sure you don't stumble and fall?

Is there anyone in your life who will fight with you? Cheer for you? Cry with you? That's why you need a small group.

I encourage you to join a small group. If you can't find one that fits your needs or schedule, start one. It's not hard to do. If you want to start a small group ask people you already feel close to and comfortable with to form one with you.

Some small groups meet for just 8-10 weeks, while others have a longer relationship. Some groups meet once a week and others meet twice a month.

It doesn't matter if you have never been involved in a small group, are a brand-new Christian or a seasoned vet—all of us are better together.

REFLECTION

- Who has your back today that will drop everything if you need them?
- Whose back do you have that you will drop everything if they need you?
- If you are not part of a small group, what is stopping you?

"The Lord is my shepherd; I have all that I need. He lets me rest in green meadows; he leads me beside peaceful streams. He renews my strength. He guides me along right paths, bringing honor to his name."

PSALM 23:1-3

DEVOTIONAL 18
PAUSE...

I like to be busy. When working outside I often have about six projects going on at the same time. When I get bored with one, I switch to another. I do this partly because it's how I'm wired. I'm an "activator" type person, so I find pleasure in filling every moment of every day, from the time I get up to the time I go to bed. Although I don't create lists just to check items off, I do feel a deep sense of fulfillment when I accomplish a task.

The other day I was meeting with my spiritual mentor when he asked me how often I take time to pause. The question didn't need clarification or explanation; we both knew exactly the point he was trying to make. My answer was, "Good question."

The truth is that I haven't been taking time to pause and contemplate. That's not because I think it isn't a worthy investment of my time—it's just that I couldn't seem to fit it into my day. At least, that is what I subconsciously thought, until the day I paused.

The day after my mentor's question I changed my morning routine. I made the kids breakfast and got them on the bus, then went and worked out. Instead of going downstairs to work on the computer or firing up some new project after coming home and showering, I paused.

We have a rocking chair upstairs in our home near a window. Usually it faces into the room, so I turned it around to face out to the field across the street. Then I sat there with a cup of coffee... and contemplated. My mentor said to take five or ten minutes just to pause and contemplate, so I set the bar high and committed to sitting still for ten minutes. (The last time I did that I was in my deer stand.)

Normally I would begin to fidget after five minutes, but this time was different. I really wanted to pause and contemplate what it means to be at peace. And dare I say it? I found it refreshing.

Since my initial pause I have not turned that chair back to the room. I have actually been practicing "the pause" several times during the week. It has been refreshing to just "be." Sometimes I read my Bible, then pause. Other times I read a devotional, then pause. I have found you can't do both at the same time (I tried).

The art of pausing for a few minutes just to contemplate the attributes of God and the realities of His presence has been amazing to practice.

I have even been able to pause while my family is at home. I just slip upstairs, close the door, pause for five minutes, and then return. My kids just think I'm in the bathroom. (By the way, pausing on the stool doesn't count.)

Who would have thought that sitting still and quiet would have propelled my spiritual life to a new depth?

Your pause may look very different than mine. You may want to pause before you head into the office for the day—just sit in the car in silence for five minutes.

REFLECTION

- Do you believe that there is a reason and a purpose for your existence?
- Is your answer based on the value put on you by others or is it based on the fact that you are already invaluable to the one and only Creator?

"Ask and it will be given to you; seek and you will find; knock and the door will be opened to you. For everyone who asks receives; he who seeks finds; and to him who knocks, the door will be opened."

MATTHEW 7:7-8

DEVOTIONAL 19
THE DOLDRUMS

Back when sailing ships ruled the seas, sailors feared The Doldrums more than anything else. It was their most dreadful situation. The Doldrums refers to parts of the Atlantic and Pacific Oceans affected by the Intertropical Convergence Zone, a low-pressure area around the equator where the prevailing winds are calm.

If a ship was slightly off-course, or The Doldrums slightly shifted they would sail into a dead zone—no winds were blowing. With no wind blowing the ship stopped moving, rendering it helpless.

Sometimes ships were stuck in The Doldrums for days or weeks. Sailors got depressed while floating in a hot, muggy climate. Many crews consumed their entire provisions and then starved to death waiting for winds that never came. If you were caught in the Doldrums and lived to tell about it, you were fortunate because many sailors never made it out alive.

The word "doldrums" is derived from "dold," an archaic term meaning "stupid," and "rum(s)," a noun suffix found in such words as "tantrum." Early sailors named this belt of no wind The Doldrums because their spirits plummeted. Today someone might say they're "in the doldrums," indicating a state of inactivity, mild depression, or feeling listless or stagnated.

God rebuked the ancient church in Laodicea because they were in the doldrums. They were neither hot nor cold—they were stuck treading water, doing nothing. God said to them, *"So, because you are lukewarm—neither hot nor cold—I am about to spit you out of my mouth."* (Revelation 3:16) The problem with this church was that they didn't realize just how lukewarm they really were.

I think that every believer drifts into the doldrums from time to time. It may be when we maybe don't really feel like living by faith, and at the same time we don't really feel like living "like we used to" (selfishly) either. It's not that we are spiritually hot or spiritually cold—we're just kind of floating, trying to hang in there for another day.

Maybe you're in the doldrums right now. Your job or relationships don't "set your sail" like they used to. It's not that you're UNhappy, but you are not happy either. It's not like you're far from God, but you certainly aren't close to Him.

What you need is a fresh wind to set your sail and blow you back on course.

The best way to catch the wind is to hoist your sail—arms up, head down, crying out for God to breathe His presence into your life.

This might seem oversimplified, but the first step IS to seek God and ask Him to blow a fresh wind your way. Jesus told his followers, *"Ask and it will be given to you; seek and you will find; knock and the door will be opened to you. For everyone who asks receives; he who seeks finds; and to him who knocks, the door will be opened."* Matthew 7:7-8

My personal prayer is that God will blow His breath of fresh air into my fragile life. I need the breath of God to lead me to where I need to be. You do too. That is my prayer for you and for me.

God called you to sail, not to sink, so seek Him now and get ready for the winds to stir.

REFLECTION

- Can you recall a time when a "fresh wind" came along and pulled you out of a doldrum in your life and if so, what did it look like? Maybe it was a new opportunity to serve, an invitation to join a small group or Bible study, a new friend that happened along at just the right time, a book that someone gave you, or a meaningful experience that inspired you to seek a new direction in your life.
- If you feel like you are in the doldrums right now, cry out to God. Ask Him to stir the wind. Hoist your sail; hoist all your sails. That is my prayer for you and for me. God called you to sail, not to sink, so seek Him now and get ready for the winds to stir.

> Do not let your hearts be troubled. Trust in God; trust also in me. In my Father's house are many rooms;
>
> **JOHN 14:1-2**

DEVOTIONAL 20
A PICTURE OF HEAVEN

Jesus was with his twelve disciples in a small upper room of someone's home. He had taken his ministry out of the public eye because the Pharisees and religious rulers planned on killing him. Then He broke the news that He was getting ready to leave them. Peter was concerned and asked Jesus where He was going. Jesus answered:

*"'Do not let your hearts be troubled. Trust in God; trust also in me. In my Father's house are many rooms; if it were not so, I would have told you. I am going there to prepare a place for you. And if I go and prepare a place for you, I will come back and take you to be with me that you also may be where I am. You know the way to the place where I am going.' Thomas said to him, 'Lord, we don't know where you are going, so how can we know the way?' Jesus answered, 'I am the way and the truth and the life. No one comes to the Father except through me.'" J*ohn 14:1-6

This is a very interesting and often misunderstood passage. Jesus says, "In my Father's house are many rooms." Some Bible translations even say "mansions." Most of the time we think of heaven from our American cultural perspective.

We think that all the homes will be lined up in a row on a nice street just like they are here. But when Jesus said that in His Father's house there were many rooms, His disciples had a different picture in mind.

In Jesus' day families lived in close proximity to each other. The family home was the center of activity where children would be raised. As they got married the girls would move in with their husband's family, which was usually just down the road.

When the boys got engaged, the father and son would begin working on an addition to the parental home to accommodate their growing family. If the family had more than one male child, they would create an addition for each son and his bride.

As the parents aged, they would trade homes, and the oldest son would get the larger home in the center. If the father had five boys the house looked more like a big apartment building than an individual dwelling.

As his kids grew up and got married, they would take the center home and this continued on and on as children were born and grandparents died.

Most homes had a center courtyard where the children played and families connected. Families also shared a central kitchen and barn that was all part of the home.

This was the picture Jesus painted for His disciples. When Jesus said that He was going to the Father to make a room for us He meant that He was going to heaven to build us a place to stay that is connected to the Father's house, and to one another.

It's a beautiful picture of a believer's eternal home in heaven based on their spiritual marriage to Christ through faith.

A biblical picture of heaven does not consist of fluffy clouds full of angels playing harps. It consists of people living together in perfect harmony, joy, and peace around the very courtyard of God.

Like Peter, believers should be comforted by Jesus' promise and look forward to laying their eyes on their Savior for the very first time.

REFLECTION

- What do you think heaven is like?
- What can we do now to make earth more like heaven?
- Reflect on the emotions you feel when you consider the day you "lay your eyes on the Savior for the first time." Are they positive or negative emotions? What does that tell you?

"A new command I give you: Love one another. As I have loved you, so you must love one another. By this everyone will know that you are my disciples, if you love one another."

JOHN 15:34-36

DEVOTIONAL 21
HELPING THOSE WHO HURT

When my then three-year-old son Joshua was diagnosed with Acute Lymphomic Leukemia I thought my life was over. He is my only son, and I love him more than words can describe. After his diagnosis, my wife Kathi and I were completely devastated and scared—struggling from day to day as we dealt with this horrible, life-changing diagnosis.

Two months into Josh's chemo the initial shock began to wear off, and a dreary reality set in. Life had changed, and we were forced to battle our precious son's disease from the sidelines.

I can't count the number of times I felt like quitting, self-medicating, eating my frustrations away, or blaming the doctors for not doing enough. I longed to retreat from the misery of our reality to the comforts of an imaginary, safe place. But I couldn't because this nightmare was real and my family, especially Josh, needed me.

Instead I made a conscious decision to trust God with every battle, every day. For the next three years Kathi and I panicked every time Josh spiked a fever, cried every time the doctors injected the horrible lifesaving chemicals into his body, and prayed for him as if it were a matter of life and death, because it was.

Finally, after three years of chemo, Josh was given a clean bill of health. Now, many years later he is an adult, still doing great, and so are we.

During those dark days I learned a lot about how healthy people respond to hurting people. I learned the nuances not talked about in textbooks or covered in college courses.

How you respond to hurting people can bring encouragement and hope, or isolation and doubt. Continue reading to learn my takeaways from this period of my life.

First—People you expect to support and encourage you night not. It's not that they don't want to; they don't know how. One of my good friends never came to the hospital, sent a Facebook message, an e-mail, or even a text asking how I was. I ran into him six months after Josh's diagnosis went public and he said he just wanted to "give me some space." If "giving space" is the same as "abandoning," he succeeded.

Sure, I could have called, but the hurt was so great and the situation so overwhelming that I could barely function and support Josh, let alone reach out.

If you know someone diagnosed with a serious illness or experiencing a serious crisis the worst thing you can do is do nothing. Just say, "I'm praying for you," or "Let me know if you need anything." Those who are hurting read every e-mail, Caring Bridge post, and letter over and over, finding strength in the faith, words, and actions of others.

Second—Sometimes people you don't know encourage you in ways you don't expect. People we hardly knew gave us food, offered to care for our daughters during doctors' visits, and even cleaned our house. This blew us away!

The outpouring of support we received from those I didn't consider to be part of my inner circle surprised me more than anything.

Third—Some people will avoid you because they think whatever is wrong with you is contagious. It seemed strange that some people avoided us. Cancer, accidents, and emotional trauma aren't contagious, so don't treat people who experience these things like they are.

Some people will avoid you because your problem is more than they can handle. Trust me, you will then run into them someplace. When you do, cough on them just for fun. And try to understand they're not trying to hurt you; they just don't know how to handle you and your problem.

Fourth—When it's over you will need to forgive some people. You will need to communicate with the people who didn't react to you as you thought they should. To this day I can remember everyone who came to see us at the hospital.

I can also remember those who never came. I had to work through my emotions because I was angry with my friends whom I thought would be there for me. I was hurt that they didn't seem to care.

I gently talked with them one by one over time and shared what I went through so they knew how I felt. I also told a couple other people who avoided me how much this hurt me; one cried, both apologized.

When I spoke with others, I simply explained our journey, hoping that by hearing of our experience they would react differently to someone else in similar circumstances. I didn't condemn them with guilt or shame. I just spoke the truth in love and prayed our relationship would be re-established.

Most of all, I had to let go and try to understand that our friends didn't intentionally mean to hurt us; they just didn't know how to react.

REFLECTION

- *If you are hurting or going through crisis right now and haven't let anyone know, will you?*
- *Ask God to bring to your mind someone who is hurting or going through crisis so that you may reach out to them in His love.*

"We remember before our God and Father your work produced by faith, your labor prompted by love, and your endurance inspired by hope in our Lord Jesus Christ."

1 THESSALONIANS 1:3

DEVOTIONAL 22
FAITH, HOPE, AND LOVE

The Apostle Paul spent three weeks in Thessalonica preaching the Gospel. A while after he returned to Athens, he sent his young disciple, Timothy, on a follow-up visit to see what was happening in the lives of the Thessalonians. Timothy came back with amazing news and said, "God is working there! It's unbelievable!" Paul was blown away with this sense of spiritual joy. So, he wrote them a letter known to us as 1 Thessalonians.

After Paul greeted them, he wrote, *"We remember before our God and Father your work produced by faith, your labor prompted by love, and your endurance inspired by hope in our Lord Jesus Christ."* 1 Thessalonians 1:3

In this one verse Paul shared three reasons he was thankful for the church in Thessalonica. First, it was because of their work produced by faith—helping their neighbors, serving others, caring for the poor. The text doesn't go into great detail about what they did exactly, Paul just spoke of their works in general.

They did these good works because they had faith in Christ. Paul states in other texts that salvation is a matter of faith, not good works. But when you have faith in Christ you are expected to take it to the streets. You share that faith through good works. It's one thing to hear how much God loves you, it's another to see God's love in action through others.

Second, Paul was thankful for their labor that was prompted by love. The love Paul is speaking about here is "agape love." The essence of agape love is goodwill and benevolence that involves faithfulness, commitment, and an act of the will. As soon as we discover what agape love is we are forced to make a decision. We either yield to that love, or we reject it. If we accept God's love, we are made new in it.

By the grace of God, we begin to see people like He seems them.

Instead of being selfish, we become self-less. Instead of seeking to receive we become more giving.

In this text Paul praises them for their agape love toward others. They understood the love of God so they willingly shared it with others. People became followers of Christ because they admired the great love they displayed.

Third, Paul was thankful for their endurance inspired by hope. Hope enables us to see setbacks as comebacks. Hope enables us to overcome even the worst of situations. The Thessalonians were being persecuted by the Jews who wanted them gone but were willing to endure trials because they had blazing hope in Christ.

Hope changes things because hope changes our perspective. The Gospel enables us to look past our current struggles and set our eyes on the hope of being with Jesus in eternity.

You may have endured immense hardships. You may have endured more pain and suffering than anyone should have to go through. Because you have endured, many people have come to see that the gospel is real.

The three key words in verse three—faith, hope, and love are seen together several times in the New Testament. That's because when we demonstrate them it makes a tangible difference in our lives and in the lives of others.

The Thessalonians were full of faith, hope, and love, and because of them disciples were made. In the same way, when we are full of faith, hope, and love, people see Jesus.

REFLECTION

- Think about which of these attributes – faith, hope, or love – is the easiest for you to demonstrate.
- How might you influence another believer to grow in their own demonstration of the attribute that is your strong suit?

> "But I have raised you up for this very purpose, that I might show you my power and that my name might be proclaimed in all the earth"
>
> **EXODUS 9:16**

DEVOTIONAL 23
CHASING A GOD-SIZE DREAM

The first night we met nobody really knew what was ahead of us. Ten men decided to use a week of vacation to build a 20 x 40-foot medical clinic from the ground up in an underserved city in Haiti. The trip was going to be hot, difficult, and demanding, but these men were willing to take these challenges because they had a deep desire to merge their God-given skills with this God-sized vision.

Our first planning meeting was when most of the guys met each other. Everyone came with their own ideas, concerns, history, challenges, and apprehensions. Since most of the men had never been to Haiti, they wanted basic information on what to expect.

Questions needed to be answered—Would there be a hardware store nearby?—Who would deliver the cement?—Would there be power?—What if it rains all week?—All are legitimate questions for beginning a construction project.

There would be no hardware store for emergencies; we have to bring our own tools, mix the mortar on site, use a small generator for power, and work in 90° heat. I thought a couple of guys might bail after finding this out, but they seemed to be intrigued by the challenge and willing to give their best efforts.

Two weeks later we flew to Port au Prince, Haiti arriving at our destination late Saturday night. Sunday, we went to worship with our sister church. We took pictures of the school Freshwater built, shook hands with a lot of new Haitian friends, and retired to bed early.

Monday morning, we were on the job site just as the sun came up to get a feel for what needed to be done. Local masons had poured the foundation and built the walls four feet high. This was a welcome sight, and unexpected. After creating an initial course of action, we prayed that God would make our time fruitful, but none of us really knew how fruitful we would actually be.

Within an hour each team member was performing a task that contributed to the goal. One man was cutting wood, another hauling block, another made cement mix. We were like a well-oiled machine. Day after day we worked in intense heat with limited supplies, and a huge language barrier.

By the end of the week the walls were up, the roof was on, and we were exhausted. Looking back, it is hard to believe we accomplished so much with so little, so fast. And once the work was done, we decided to relax at the beach for our last half day there.

While at the beach we had one last huddle to share our experiences from the day. One person shared how God met them in a profound way that week, another talked about the joy of serving the poorest of the poor. A third person confessed to learning to trust God with all the details. Ultimately, we paused long enough to celebrate the win.

We had done what seemed like an impossible task. What began as a pile of blocks had turned into a two-room medical clinic. This was a big win for the ten of us men, for the church, and ultimately for the thousands of people this clinic will serve.

This team and our efforts for God's glory will never fade away. I was challenged and encouraged by every person on the team. What began as a random group of men who dreamed that God could use them in a big way, turned into a band of brothers who accomplished the dream God set before them. They believed that God could and would use them in a profound way if they were willing, and He did!

Today the Haitian workers have the building finished and ready for use. Lives are being saved and the Gospel is being shared. All because 10 men caught the dream and chased it.

"But I have raised you up for this very purpose, that I might show you my power and that my name might be proclaimed in all the earth."

Exodus 9:16

REFLECTION

- *What are you truly passionate about?*
- *If God removed all the obstacles from your path, what would you be doing to advance his kingdom?*

"If anyone is thirsty, let him come to me and drink. Whoever believes in me, as the Scripture has said, streams of living water will flow from within him."

JOHN 7:37-38

DEVOTIONAL 24
LIVING WATER

In Deuteronomy God commanded the Israelites to celebrate the Feast of Tabernacles by building small functional booths called "Sukkot" which were made of olive, palm, and myrtle branches. The booths provided shade during the week-long celebration and were also very symbolic to the Israelites.

Right in the middle of the roof they left a hole enabling sight of clear blue sky during the day and light from the temple at night. For seven days the people lived, ate, and slept in the Sukkot booths erected throughout Jerusalem. It was a time to praise God for the past gifts of freedom, land, and bountiful harvests.

Water was an important part of the festival. Quality water was hard to come by since most water came out of cisterns or wells. It was drinkable but tasted terrible.

Running water from rainfalls, streams, or rivers was different than water from a cistern or well because it never went stagnant or stale. It was so special that people called running water "living water" because it tasted fresh. During the feast people celebrated the "living water" that God provided them.

The Feast of Tabernacles, also called the Sukkot Festival took place at the end of the dry season. Rains were needed immediately afterward to ensure a harvest the following year, so the priests added a ceremony that included a prayer for rain.

This part of the ceremony involved a procession of priests accompanied by flutes, marching from the temple to the Pool of Siloam which was fed by the Spring of Gihon. There, one of the priests filled a golden pitcher with living water out of the Pool of Siloam and the procession returned to the temple.

The priest carrying the pitcher entered the priests' court through the

Water Gate and with a blast of the shofar (a musical horn produced from a ram's horn) he approached the altar where sacrifices were laid.

He made one circle around the altar as the crowd sang the *Hallel* which is Psalm 113-118. While reading 118:25-27 they waved *lulavim*, palm branches with the leaves tied up. The people waved them with passion and excitement while shouting the verses.

"Lord, save us! Lord, grant us success! Blessed is he who comes in the name of the Lord. From the house of the Lord we bless you. The Lord is God, and he has made his light shine on us." Psalm 118:25-27

Then the priest climbed the ramp and stood near the top of the altar. He poured the water down two silver funnels leading into the stone altar for the daily drink offerings. As he poured the water the crowds chanted "Hosanna! Hosanna! Hosanna!" which means "Lord save us."

The symbolism here is powerful. They were singing "Hosanna, Hosanna, Blessed is He who comes in the name of the LORD!" having no idea that the Messiah was with them. He had come!

On the last and greatest day of the feast, in the middle of the water ceremony the chanted prayers, and the plea through the offering of living water Jesus stood up in the crowd and declared,

"If anyone is thirsty, let him come to me and drink. Whoever believes in me, as the Scripture has said, streams of living water will flow from within him." John 7:37-38

Jesus declared that in a spiritual sense He is the living water that people desperately need. He tied the symbolism to Himself because He is the only way, He is the living water. In a physical sense you and I need water to live and in a spiritual sense we need Jesus to live. Jesus came to quench our spiritual thirst. The thirst for answers ends at the cross.

REFLECTION

- What qualities does water have that make it the perfect parallel to Christ in this biblical analogy?
- Take a moment to really reflect on the beautiful imagery you see here and ask God to offer up opportunities to experience this same beauty in your own life.

> "I consider that our present sufferings are not worth comparing with the glory that will be revealed in us."
>
> **ROMANS 8:18**

DEVOTIONAL 25
THE TUMBLER

There are times when I get discouraged, thinking I should be farther ahead in my Christian life than I am. Sometimes I become frustrated because I need to be patient and hold my tongue, yet I say things I wish I hadn't. However, my new hobby has reminded me that I am a work in progress and sometimes that progress takes a while.

I have always wanted a rock polisher and recently a friend of mine bought one for my birthday. I like how polished rocks feel in my hand and enjoy admiring their beauty. But I had no idea that polishing a rock took so long!

To start the process, you need to find the right rocks. You want rocks that have color and character, two things that make them worth viewing. Then you need to make sure these rocks are the right size. If they are too big the abrasive won't work; but if they are too small, they just disintegrate.

After selecting the rocks that are the right color, character, and size, you put them in the tumbler, add the coarse abrasive and water, and let the rocks tumble against one another for seven to ten days.

When this process is over, you wash the rocks, put them back in the tumbler with a medium grip abrasive and let them tumble for another week. After the second tumble is over, you rinse them, add a fine abrasive grit, and tumble them for another week or so.

When the rocks feel smooth you rinse them, add polish to the tumbler, and let them roll for another week. Finally, you rinse them yet again and tumble them with soap for a day.

By the time this whole process was over; it had taken me five weeks to polish a handful of rocks!

God is in the polishing business. When we become Christians, we are rough around the edges and have unpolished lives. Our language might be colorful, our choice of clothing a little provocative, and our hearts may need some correction.

But over time God patiently works in our lives through people and circumstances, smoothing out the rough spots—because He sees the gem inside. The biblical word for this is "sanctification." It implies us submitting to God's will and in the process becoming more holy.

Sometimes this process can be painful, but the end result is worth it. When we allow God to sanctify us, He will smooth out the rough edges and we will emerge polished, beautiful and more like Him.

If you feel like your spiritual life isn't where it should be right now, be patient. Trust that God will continue to smooth out your rough spots and take off your sharp edges making you even more beautiful inside than you already are. Stay strong and press on. God isn't finished with you yet.

REFLECTION

- What "rough edge" has already been smoothed out by God's presence in your life?
- What God-given character traits are shining through more and more as God polishes you through sanctification?
- Is there a character trait that you wish would shine through more? Trust that it will as you submit to becoming more holy.

"I am the light of the world. Whoever follows me will never walk in darkness but will have the light of life."

JOHN 8:12

DEVOTIONAL 26
THE LIGHT OF THE WORLD

Imagine this: Jesus is in the temple in the center of Jerusalem standing near massive torches, called Menorahs. There were four of these seven-headed torches that stood 75 feet high in an area inside the temple walls. This area of the temple was a common gathering space for the people. It separated the men's area from the women's area.

Here in this room, positioned directly next to a torch that burns all night long during the Feast of Tabernacles, Jesus declared that He is the light of the world, *"I am the light of the world. Whoever follows me will never walk in darkness but will have the light of life."* John 8:12

There is significant symbolism here. The Menorah flames were positioned at the highest point in Jerusalem and the Holy Land and burned so brightly at night that they would be seen all over the region.

When Jesus said, "I am the Light of the World," His people understood the importance of His claim. They knew Jesus was claiming to be their deliverer.

From this point on the Menorahs were more than just light to the dark of the night. They symbolized the glory of the Lord that filled the temple while the Jews were in the desert. They symbolized the guidance that is offered from the Holy Spirit—the Light in our darkest days.

Christ is literally fulfilling all of the spiritual truths that the symbolism of the festival implied.

- He claimed to be the Bread of Life in John 6 like the Manna was life to the Jews.
- He claimed to be the Living Water in a spiritual sense in John 7, like fresh water is to the body.

� Now He claims to be the Light of the World in John 8, symbolizing the pillar of fire that guided the Israelites in the desert.

REFLECTION

- *Are you letting Jesus be the light in your life and guide you?*
- *If you believe that Jesus is the light of the world are you offering His light in your life to others to find hope and healing in Christ?*

> "My sheep listen to my voice; I know them, and they follow me."
>
> **JOHN 10:27**

DEVOTIONAL 27
THE HOLY SPIRIT'S VOICE

My friend Tom told me about an experience he had while in Norway visiting his friend Johan. As a shepherd Johan needed to bring his sheep a salt block. Tom had the opportunity to go to the pasture with him.

They drove to a grassy hill that was an excellent pasture for the sheep. Several farmers in the area use the same grazing land, and the sheep were gathered in multiple groups along the hill.

Johan walked out into the field with the salt block, then called out, "Come here my little sheep; come here my little sheep." His sheep immediately recognized his voice and came running toward him.

All the other sheep acted as if they didn't hear a thing and continued to graze. Incredible, right? It is the same way with recognizing the Holy Spirit's voice.

As we know, Jesus, the Father, and the Holy Spirit are one (2 Corinthians 13:14). The more you know Jesus, the more you will be able to recognize the Holy Spirit's voice in your life.

Get to know His voice through His word, His people, circumstances, and the gentle nudge in your heart when you pray.

The Holy Spirit will be your guide in following Christ's lead. Jesus was sent here in human form—God/man—so that we could identify with Him. Although it can seem overwhelming to imagine living like Jesus in every area of our life, this is what God enables us to do.

By following Christ's example, we will be better in our relationships, more effective at sharing the gospel, and most importantly, we will be honoring God at every crossroad.

Here's a suggestion to guide you in recognizing the Holy Spirit's voice—The Holy Spirit speaks in alignment with God's attributes. God will never contradict himself.

- God will never whisper that you need to have an affair or spend your entire check on lottery tickets.
- He will never tell you to harm someone or take revenge on a person that recently harmed you.

You may wonder if it's the Holy Spirit prompting you, but it's not. God will confirm His whisper with His Word written in the Bible.

Anything that contradicts His Word is not from The Holy Spirit because God isn't making up new rules just for your situation. If you think He is, check again, because He's not.

Another suggestion is to seek the opinion of trusted, Christ-following friends.

- If you feel like you are being called to lead a specific ministry, do they see that for your life?
- If you feel you are being prompted to financially support a specific ministry, would these trusted friends agree that this is a God-thing?

REFLECTION

- In the context of this devotion, what are the good things about being a sheep? What are the negatives?
- What steps can you take to ensure you follow the right shepherd?

> "Every branch that does bear fruit he prunes so that it will be even more fruitful."
>
> **JOHN 15:2**

DEVOTIONAL 28
CONNECTED TO THE VINE

Every year there is only a two-month window when Mount Everest can be climbed. The rest of the year the winds are so fierce and the temperatures so low that it is considered impossible to climb. It can cost a climber up to $70,000 to attempt to summit Mount Everest. Thousands of people have sold their cars, homes, and/or personal belongings for a shot at reaching the top.

Gerard McDonnell was one of these people. He paid a huge price for his attempt to reach the summit. As he was scaling the mountain his trip leader warned him to turn around because his hands and feet were severely frostbitten. Gerard refused to listen.

After hiking further up the mountain Gerard realized he wouldn't make it without permanent physical damage and he finally turned around. Unfortunately, this decision came too late.

Gerard had such severe frostbite that every finger on one hand, the majority of fingers on the other hand, and half of one of his feet had to be amputated after his attempted climb.

The truth is, Jesus doesn't really care if you climb to the top of the world or not. He isn't into expeditions where one tries to "tame" the North Pole or "conquer" the jungle.

Jesus never said, "If you really want your life to count, then climb the highest mountain or swim the across the coldest ocean." Jesus tells us that if we want our life to really count, stay really close to Him and He will produce spiritual fruit.

"I am the vine; you are the branches. If a man remains in me and I in him, he will bear much fruit; apart from me you can do nothing. If anyone does not remain in me, he is like a branch that is thrown away and withers; such branches are picked up, thrown into the fire and burned." John 15:5

The key to remaining in Christ is to obey His commands. And to be successfully obedient, you need to let God prune your life. According to Jesus, *"Every branch that does bear fruit he prunes so that it will be even more fruitful."* (John 15:2)

I need the Holy Spirit to prune my life on a regular basis so that spiritual fruits such as love, joy, peace, patience, gentleness, and self-control can be produced in my life (Galatians 5:22-23).

- If you have no margin in your life ask Jesus to help you prune your calendar.
- If you have someone in your life who is dragging you down and leading you away from Christ ask Jesus to help prune them from your life.
- If you have distractions or addictions that keep your gaze away from the Cross ask for pruning to take place.

The cool thing is, when we let God prune our lives our faith grows. I trust Jesus now more than ever because He cut things out of my life that I didn't think I could give up. Now I can see how His pruning produced spiritual fruit.

Jesus says, *"You did not choose me, but I chose you and appointed you so that you might go and bear fruit—fruit that will last—and so that whatever you ask in my name the Father will give you."* John 15:16

Becoming fruit-bearing is the result of staying connected to Jesus, the Vine. You may never be a CEO, President of the United States, a famous musician, or climb Mount Everest.

But I promise, if you let God do a little pruning and if you remain in Jesus, the Holy Spirit will produce fruit in your life. This pruning will inevitably spread the Gospel and last into eternity.

REFLECTION

- What are one or two spiritual fruits that might not be growing so well?
- Now that you think about it, can you recognize some prompts you have had to allow some pruning?

> "I know that my Redeemer lives, and that in the end he will stand upon the earth."
>
> **JOB 19:25**

DEVOTIONAL 29
SUFFERING

Sometimes suffering is only temporary, like when we need to get a dental cavity filled. It only hurts while you're in the chair, then the pain goes away. Other times suffering lasts longer—for days, months, or even years. In these times of suffering we can persevere by clinging to the hope we have in Christ.

Job is a great biblical example of a person who endured intense suffering. All Job's animals were killed or stolen, his servants and children were killed, and his body was covered with horrible sores from the top of his head to the bottom of his feet. He was an emotional wreck and in physical pain. Job shared his emotions in chapter three.

"After this, Job opened his mouth and cursed the day of his birth. He said: "May the day of my birth perish, and the night it was said, 'A boy is born!' That day—may it turn to darkness; may God above not care about it; may no light shine upon it." Job 3:1-4

Job's friends didn't understand what he was going through. Although they offered a few pieces of good advice they offered bad advice more often. They falsely determined that Job's afflictions were caused by sin.

The truth is, Job wasn't suffering because he sinned. He was suffering because in this life we will encounter suffering at times. Job didn't need an inaccurate diagnosis as to why this was happening; he needed hope to persevere through it.

We can't expect others to understand our suffering and respond empathetically all of the time. Sometimes friends say hurtful words truly intended to help. In reality they simply may not understand.

Shortly after Josh was diagnosed with leukemia, I had breakfast with a friend. As he sat across from me at a restaurant, he proceeded to tell me that Josh was sick because of my sin—that I didn't spiritually protect my family! His words hurt me so much that I had to get counseling—his words cut like a knife. Job could have had similar feelings. Words like this lay unnecessary guilt on someone who is already suffering.

If you are in a position to respond to someone's suffering—

- make friendship your first priority—your presence means more than your words.
- Second, bring comfort and not condemnation, by resisting the temptation to diagnose the situation in a way that lays blame.
- Third, bring encouragement, not discouragement. Be present, and care for the person who is suffering.

Job was able to persevere because he recognized God as his savior and redeemer. "*I know that my Redeemer lives, and that in the end he will stand upon the earth.*" Job 19:25 He knew that God is the One who will provide for him regardless of how much he suffers or how long he suffers.

Job professed that even if God himself was causing this, he would still hope in Him because one day he will see God face to face. Some of us will never understand why we are suffering. Our only hope is to trust Jesus, persevere, and look forward to being in the presence of the Almighty King where all things will be revealed.

REFLECTION

- Reflect on a time that you have suffered intensely (or imagine a scenario of suffering).
- With that reflection in mind, what thoughts or feelings arise as you read the statement, "Job professed that even if God Himself was causing this, he would still hope in Him because one day he will see God face to face."?

> "I am the resurrection and the life. Anyone who believes in me will live, even after dying. Everyone who lives in me and believes in me will never, ever die."
>
> **JOHN 11:25-26**

DEVOTIONAL 30
BELIEVE

From the beginning to the end of the Gospel of John the word "believe" is written 43 times. It is clearly a key word in this book. *"But these are written that you may believe that Jesus is the Christ, the Son of God, and that by believing you may have life in his name."* John 20:31

When you believe in something you are all in. My 13-year-old daughter Katie and I took a trip to Grand Marais to go snowmobiling. We stayed in a hotel right on Lake Superior. Katie is rather adventurous and she said, "Dad, I want to do the polar plunge." Being the good father that I am I said, "Have fun! I'll watch you from the shore."

She put on her bathing suit and wrapped herself in a towel, and we headed down to Lake Superior. As she stood by the side of the lake Katie was talking and talking and talking about going all the way in for an entire minute. A couple out for a walk heard Katie and said, "Well, are you going in or not?" After another minute of waiting they left.

Katie turned to me and asked if the water would be cold and I said, "Of course it's cold! It's Lake Superior in the winter!" After another 30 seconds of debating she gave a shout, yelling, "I'm going all the way in, Dad! Watch me!" And watch her I did.

Katie took two steps into the icy water, and by the time it reached her ankles she screamed and hollered that she was freezing. Immediately she ran from the water, back to the hotel.

In the same way that Katie had every intention of going all the way into that icy water, Jesus tells us to go all in. We can't just stick our toes in the shallow end of the spiritual pool. Jesus invites us to jump in the deep end.

It is critical for our spiritual walk that we not just acknowledge, but wholeheartedly believe God. This firm belief is the root of all our decisions, and it guides us in our actions like a compass.

God doesn't expect you to have it all together or maintain a perfect track record in order to jump in. He invites you to believe right now, just as you are.

Jesus promised, *"I am the resurrection and the life. Anyone who believes in me will live, even after dying. Everyone who lives in me and believes in me will never, ever die."* John 11:25-26

Do you believe these words?

REFLECTION

- *Have you found yourself guilty of pushing off the decision to go all in because you don't have it all together yet?*
- *How did that play out? Was it worth the wait?*
- *If you have not yet accepted Christ as your Savior, pray for God to reveal to you any road blocks you may not yet recognize as something that's keeping you from going all in.*

"The King will reply, 'Truly I tell you, whatever you did for one of the least of these brothers and sisters of mine, you did for me.'"

MATTHEW 25:40

DEVOTIONAL 31
THREE SPIRITUAL CATALYSTS

There are three universal spiritual catalysts that seem to keep our hearts ready and willing to make spiritual progress. They are not radical or crazy, just solid principles that help us make progress. I urge you to take responsibility to do these because they will help you grow.

1. **Attend church every week.** When we get together with other believers to celebrate what God is doing, something about that activity helps us stay connected to Christ. Schedule going to church every week on your calendar. That will help you avoid being tempted to fill in the time with something else. This time of worship and fellowship is critical to our spiritual growth.

2. **Participate in a group.** I love my small group because they challenge me and hold me accountable. We usually eat together, study together, and pray together. You need to participate in a group to experience true Christian fellowship. A wise man once said, "Everyone needs to sit at a table where nobody is impressed with you." This way you can be real and they can be real. Together you can glorify God through fellowship.

3. **Serve others.** The third catalyst is serving others. One time while serving at a local homeless shelter God taught me a profound lesson on serving. After leading a worship service and feeding many people, we would also clean the facility.

   One time I was asked to clean the men's bathroom and it smelled really bad. I think the fan was broken that night. While I was scrubbing the toilet and gagging, I started asking myself why I was doing this job.

   Immediately God nudged my heart and said, "Because you came to serve and that's exactly what you need to do." It was a humbling moment, and I never resisted cleaning the toilets after that.

   When we serve others it reminds us that we are not the center of the universe. And when we serve others we are serving Jesus. *"The King will reply, 'Truly I tell you, whatever you did for one of the least of these brothers and sisters of mine, you did for me."* Matthew 25:40

Believers serve an amazing, incredible, awesome, glorious heavenly Father who loves us so much that He sacrificed His son Jesus Christ, for our sins. For that reason, we need to take responsibility for our faith. Putting these three spiritual catalysts into action in our lives is a great place to start.

REFLECTION

- What is the roadblock that most often keeps you from attending church on a given Sunday? What can you do to get around it next time?
- Whether you are currently in a small group or not, reflect on the fact that there is group of believers in our church that needs the dynamic that only you can bring to their group.
- Did you recently hear of an opportunity to serve and haven't responded? Why?

NOTES

NOTES

NOTES

NOTES

NOTES

NOTES

NOTES

ABOUT THE AUTHOR
JOHN BRALAND

Growing up in Minnesota, John joined the United States Air Force after high school serving in the U.S. and abroad. After being honorably discharged, he attended Crown College where he met Kathi and married her a year later. John and Kathi have three awesome children: Josh, Sara, Katie; two black labs; and two noisy parakeets. John enjoys riding his Harley and snowmobile, tinkering on a zillion projects in the garage, playing hockey, and mentoring other leaders.

John serves as the President of International Ministerial Fellowship (IMF), a global organization with over 1,300 members that include military chaplains, pastors, parachurch workers, and missionaries. In his role with IMF, he is able to mentor other leaders and consult with churches helping them to make disciples and strengthen leaders.

John has a B.A. in Pastoral Ministry and an M.A. in Organizational Leadership from Crown College. He also earned a Doctorate of Ministry in Executive Leadership for Larger Organizations from Bethel University. He is ordained with the Christian and Missionary Alliance and with International Ministerial Fellowship.

ALSO BY JOHN BRALAND

IT IS POSSIBLE FOR YOU TO HEAL FROM YOUR WOUNDS AND THRIVE AGAIN!

Everyone has been wounded in some way, shape, or form, but most people never actually heal. Don't let your wounds keep you from experiencing the joy-filled life that God has for you. Gain the tools you need to break free from negative thought cycles so you can move from feeling wounded to enjoying wonderful.

WOUNDED
to
WONDERFUL

a biblically-based approach for finding emotional healing, hope, and happiness in your life

DR. JOHN BRALAND

Available at Amazon.com
ISBN 978-1-7341023-2-1

Made in the USA
Monee, IL
02 July 2020